A Valued Barber from Sicily

UN PREZIOSO BARBIERE SICILIANO

MICHAEL J FLAGG

CONTENTS

PROLOGUE

Having already completed two full length biographies, the inevitable question is why undertake this one? Unlike a novel, there is no direct personal identification of the biographer's involvement except to do the research and collate what, in their view as the writer, is important historically and hopefully of compelling interest to the intended reader. Consequently, as with any other biography, many questions arose at the outset of this project – the primary one being 'What was the purpose of writing it? Who is the intended audience and what are they likely to gain from reading it?'

At the foundation surely must be the motivation of the biographer to highlight and stimulate interest in the biographical subject. This writer has known Santo Raia, for over fifty years having been one of his many clients since his days starting in Proctor Street, Holborn, London. Surely from a customer's perspective the importance of hairdressing is, as these pages will hopefully convey, to have confidence and trust in the provider of the service.

Santo originates from the largest island in the Mediterranean which itself has a fascinating and compelling history and has recently been the subject of an impressive TV documentary series presented by Professor Michael Scott. It has also attracted authors such as Jeremy Dummett, creator of 'Syracuse City of Legends', and John Julius Norwich whose 'Sicily a Short History from the Ancient Greeks to Cosa Nostra', published in 2015 is masterfully entertaining, comprehensive and excellently researched.

What has been an educational journey for this writer is the contribution of many from the Italian Peninsula as a whole to the British economy over time, but in this case more specifically of those from Sicily which has some major differences. In addition, there is the attraction of the human story of any immigrant coming to a foreign country, starting up and running a business, creating a family and surviving, especially in the unpredictable field of hairdressing in London, all of which requires courage as well as personal conviction.

On reading this short work about Santo, it is hoped that the appreciation of his form of art will survive and continue to grow despite the ravages of the recent lockdowns and the major questions about its future which it shares in common with other service industries.

INTRODUCTION
ARE HAIR STYLISTS UNDERVALUED IN THE UK?

How much do you value your hairdresser? The first wave of the coronavirus outbreak, which forced the cessation of the activities of hairdressers for three months, actually served to emphasise and enhance the importance of hairdressing to most of the general public. Whereas in the corridors of power it is an essential at a price that might not be justifiably affordable by the majority, Harry Wallop, in the Daily Telegraph of January 2014, attempts to dispel any assumption that hairdressing is unimportant. He cites certain British prime ministers as all having had a head of hair, although Winston Churchill is not mentioned. Apparently, David Cameron's bald patch was skilfully covered up by his hairdresser, Lino Carboniferous, who was subsequently awarded an MBE in the 2019 New Year's Honours List! The Queen's hairstylist, Ian Carmichael, of the Dorchester Hotel's Royston Blyth salon, received a royal warrant and Jo Hanford, hair colourist to the Duchess of Cornwall, an MBE.

Awards such as these surely serve to emphasise the importance of the hairdresser who is regarded in a situation of trust and closeness to persons in positions of power and influence. Stage and cinema have make-up artists who serve to raise the credibility of a performer and not merely for vanity, but as a means of enhancing the image of someone in public life, whether male or female, whether in the House of Commons or the Boardroom. As well as appearance, personal service occupations such as medicine, law, hospitality, hairdressing itself and, of course, politics depend upon a confident array of interpersonal skills as well as appearance. Also required is the application of technology, or nuances to deliver a style the customer needs in order to change or maintain that person's image. This might entail using a combination of techniques such as hair colouring, hair cutting and hair texturing. To do this, most hairdressers are professionally licensed as either a hairdresser, a barber or a cosmetologist.

It has been said that hairdressers become multifaceted personalities since they do not simply develop one set of skills. Not only is there always something new to learn in terms of technique but also, every customer is different, which necessitates a constantly changing approach to deliver a personalised service at every level. When dealing with people from different personal, cultural and professional backgrounds, it cannot simply be about the hair and the scalp, for hairdressers also need to communicate effectively in accordance with their clients' personalities. The successful professional even learns to adapt to an individual's moods and emotions and becomes a better communicator by understanding and responding more closely to that customer's specific priorities.

In taking responsibility for their work, the hairdresser has a direct impact on the salon's revenue and profitability and this is reason enough to cultivate expertise and tailor services to match individual preferences. The rewards, of course, are beyond mere financial returns – they become well-rounded people with not only hairdressing expertise, but also the ability to interact with confidence and sensitivity towards clients, exhibiting the air of a successful and independent professional.

According to 'Ancient Hairdressing Europe', the first famous hairdresser was Champagne, who was born in Southern France and moved to Paris to open his own salon where he dressed the hair of wealthy Parisian women until his death in 1658.

In the seventeenth century, women's hair grew taller in style as popularised by Madame Martin. Further back in time, hairdressers seem to appear with civilization itself, with the exception being that Egyptian deities included a barber god. Comparatively little is known about history's earliest hairdressers who curled the beards of Sumerian princes and built the fabulous headdresses of Egyptian princesses. The market squares of ancient Greek cities had barbershops where people could laze and gossip.

Roman towns also contained hairdressing salons, visited mostly by the middle classes, while slaves dressed the heads of upper-class women. Such practices also survived in the Byzantine east. (Source: Hairdressers Today)

In AD 1000 in monasteries, the barber-surgeon, not a physician, would care for soldiers during and after the battle. This involved anything from cutting hair to amputating limbs and pulling teeth, resulting in mortality often through blood loss. By contrast, physicians regarded themselves as a cut above these functions through seeking academia in universities or living in castles and only treating the wealthy. In Britain, formal recognition of barbering skills dates from 1540 when professionalism was recognised through a Fellowship gained by way of apprenticeship rather than academia. In 1745, the surgeons split from the barbers to form the Company of Surgeons, and, in 1800, a Royal Charter was created. Thereafter, few links remained between surgery and barbering except the red and white barber's pole representing the blood and bandages associated with surgery.

Having now read this introduction, it might be a surprise for the reader to learn that hairdressing, in the UK as a whole, is not regarded by the public at large as a profession. Its importance rests with any individual who seeks to look good for that special date, or perhaps, for a majority of men especially, merely for hair maintenance. Trends come and go and in recent times, some young men seem to have favoured a shaven head, perhaps because they expect to go bald anyway, or perhaps because it requires zero hair maintenance, or simply as the imitation of a role model. Arguments have also been made that a shaven head actually stimulates new and vigorous growth, so it is a good idea for the longer term. As well as being a personal service, hair styling, in the same way as clothing, is subject to continuously changing trends in fashion, which brings us to why this short work about Santo Raia from Calamonaci in Sicily, who has spent over sixty years in the City of London, was created – for he is 'A Unique Sicilian Hair Stylist of Distinction!' (Un unico siciliano di hair stylist di distinzione!) offering a unique scissor cut for a reasonable price!

What is a Sicilian?

According to Veronica Di Grigoli, author and translator, who has worked internationally and now lives in the Sicilian capital, Palermo, it was the medieval Arabs and Normans who, as rulers, created the modern Sicily of today. From their desert origins, the Africans built potteries, factories and underground irrigation channels. They brought in crops and citrus trees to create the lush 'paradise' promised by the Koran in the afterlife.

They invented pasta and brought it to Sicily in the fifth century, contrary to the notion that it originated in China, even though noodles can be traced back there to 3000 BC and ice cream to 200 BC. Today, in Trapani, there is a large pasta factory making 'Poiatti'.

After the introduction of ceramics and textiles, Sicily became one of the world's richest trading places. The cities founded over the island had city walls and fortresses to protect them, mosques, public baths, markets and local government offices. Vikings from the frozen north, who established themselves in France and became the 'Normans', would eventually travel much further south to take over the island of Sicily. Its history can be traced back 3000 years and humans have inhabited it for 12,000. The island has been influenced by the invasions of different cultures from the Ancient Greeks, the Romans, Vandals, Ostrogoths, Byzantines and Arabs, all of whom made contributions to its art, architecture and cuisine. Some of this history can be evidenced from cave drawings in North West Sicily and the island's seven UNESCO World Heritage Sites. This book will return to these features/topics in greater depth at a later stage.

It is assumed that the Muslims were allowed to stay due to their religious tolerance and advanced agricultural techniques. The Jews were regarded as literate members of society who could draw up contracts and also had an understanding of the Egyptians and Arabs, thereby having a significant influence on the development of the island. The municipality of Calamonaci in the province of Agrigento, the birthplace of Santo Raia, the subject of this book, is 125 kilometres south of Palermo in the South East of Sicily and is known for cultivated almonds, olives, grapes, honey, citrus fruits and an extra virgin oil called 'biancolilla'. In addition, there are cattle breeding and crafts such as broom and breadbasket-making and hand-woven wicker baskets, known as 'Coffe'.

Two views of Ribera in the province of Agrigento where Santo was born.

SANTO'S CHILDHOOD HOME IN CALAMONACI

At the front door today.

Upper floors of Santo's childhood home.

Santo recalled that he went to school when he was six years old, and, on the fifth day, was required to work in his father's hairdressing salon part-time on Wednesday and Saturday afternoons, mainly making the lather with which his father would shave his clients. His elder brother also helped by doing his father's office work. That his father had a range of skills including shoemaking and was very strict gave rise to the idea that he had little affection for his sons. However, it wasn't until after his father had died that the opposite was revealed. Santo feels he had a happy childhood and that his mother amicably ran the house. Most of the local population were farmers although there were also some doctors. After the death of their father, Santo's elder brother continued with the hairdressing business for three years, after which Santo was to take his 'Terza Media' (compulsory school examinations), which he failed. Although his brother found a private tutor, Santo showed little interest in completing his studies which were to be followed by compulsory military service, something that he did not relish. Consequently, because he had a sister and a brother-in-law living in Killick Street, King's Cross in London, who had emigrated in 1952, he also took the decision to leave for England and he arrived in June 1960. At that time, you had to have the offer of a job before you could do this and it was here that his brother-in-law, now in London, was to help him. Italian families are renowned for being very supportive of one other and his brother-in-law had become 'in the know' about suitable jobs which might come up through his circle of contacts. Santo sought a position in either hairdressing or catering and catering came up first.

This position was as a temporary waiter at the Punchbowl & Ladle, a breakfast pub way down in Polperro, Cornwall, where he worked from July 1st to September 1st 1960.

The reasons behind Santo's decision to come to London for employment would not be dissimilar to those of others from the Italian

Peninsula in previous times. This, of course, includes others from Britain's former colonies. Santo's experience in London, which began in September 1960, will be detailed later following a review of some of the history of overseas workers who came to England.

Some History of Immigration from the Italian Peninsula.

For instance, this immigration covers the many people from Emilia Romagna (capital, Bologna) who had come to London through existing family ties. In the 19th century, this became known as 'chain migration', to the 'Italian colony of Clerkenwell', which had established itself in the catering industry through running classic fish and chip shops and workmen's cafés. People who came from Emilia Romagna, perhaps owing to the lack of employment opportunities in their own country, had been guaranteed a place to live and work in order that they would be issued with a four-year work permit by the Home Office. It is also the case that an even larger number of Italians emigrated to the United States, especially to New York, in search of a new life.

Significant in Santo's case was that his brother-in-law was working for London Bricks in Bedford, which, in itself, is another interesting example of how Italian immigrants, amongst others, were employed and made a significant contribution to the economy at that time. The daily journey from King's Cross to Bedford was an easy commute by train and London Bricks was known as a paternalistic enterprise with excellent working conditions, including a week's paid holiday implemented in 1930. There were sports and recreational facilities for staff and other benefits such as staff welfare, pension and profit-sharing schemes, similar to Cadbury's Bourneville in Birmingham. All this was found in an enterprise that had dominated brick production for most of the twentieth century, since its foundation in 1889 by entrepreneur J. C. Hill in Fletton, Huntingdonshire. It had several works throughout the country emerging from Peterborough with Oxford Clay as its natural resource.

Although the number of brickworks had declined between 1900 and 1930, Fletton remained a successful enterprise thanks to cost advantages.

During the Second World War, production continued with the employment of a female workforce. Post-1945, due to the lack of British nationals returning to the brick factory, they were replaced by a small number of prisoners of war from local farms as well as displaced persons from Poland and the Ukraine. By 1955, 92% of Italian male migrants, of which Santo's brother-in-law was one, had arrived on brickwork contracts and of the 783 who arrived that year, 468 (60%) stayed.

Sadly, the cost of leases, as well as the commercial value of cafés and other buildings in London, would increase, which would spell the end of the affordable cafés run by Italians and a restaurant culture for manual workers especially. Also, the first generation of Italian immigrants during this period would have achieved some social mobility and begun to move out of 'Little Italy' in Clerkenwell to the more prosperous boroughs of Finchley and Southgate, which later, Santo would also do. However, the Italian church of St Peter's in Clerkenwell would remain a focus in that community, especially the procession of St Mary of Carmel, which had taken place around the church on the third Sunday of July since 1883.

Even today, Italians in London are still actively involved in associations that directly relate to their regions of origin, as well as the activities supported by the Italian church. It is also significant that Santo and his wife Marianna chose to be married in this beautiful church in Clerkenwell's 'Little Italy' on August 20th 1961. This was the culmination of a five-year engagement that began in 1957 when Santo was eighteen. He was from Calamonaci and Marianna from Ribera. Santo had first caught sight of Marianna on a bus with her mother, and, when they all got off in Calamonaci, Santo took courage and introduced himself. It must have been especially difficult when Santo came to England in September 1960 as they would be separated for a whole year until their wedding day.

Outside St Peter's Cathedral in Clerkenwell at the
Wedding of Santo and Marianna.

Cake Cutting for the Happy Couple.

The wedding service of Santo and Marianna.

Inside St Peter's Italian Church in Clerkenwell Road, London EC1.
(*Courtesy of Alamy*)

Outside St Peter's Church in Clerkenwell Road, London EC1.

Other wedding photos.

After their marriage, Santo and Marianna would live at 109 Caledonian Road, London N7, which was a rented flat and their first home. In 1972, they would move to their current and long-term house in Southgate.

A Review of Other Historical Reasons for Italian Immigration

In previous ages, deprivation may have encouraged emigration from European areas such as Southern Italy, Sicily and Sardinia, especially if there were large numbers of landless peasants and a prevalence of malnutrition and disease. Much further back, in AD 43, the invasion by Julius Caesar at Deal in Kent was regarded as the first invasion from the Italian Peninsula, although within five centuries, 50,000 Roman soldiers had settled in Britain in the Celtic Christian areas where trading prevailed. Lombard Street in London owed its designation to Lombardy in northern Italy and the merchants and bankers from there in AD 1000. Also, there was a group of bankers, together with a group of financiers from the Italian Peninsula, with whom Edward 1 negotiated to borrow money for projects in Britain. Other bankers such as Frescobaldi financed ventures for numerous members of royal families in some other European countries. Examples of Italian influence in Britain can also be traced back to mediaeval times through the construction of the 'Cosmati Pavement'; an inlaid pavement created by a family of craftsmen who specialised in this type of work and who contributed to the reconstruction of Westminster Abbey in 1245.

Fernand Braudel highlighted the 'Financial conquest of England' as the greatest achievement of Florentine firms, who not only held the purse-strings of the kings of England but also controlled sales of English wool which was to become essential to continental workshops. Another historian, Alwyn Ruddock, claimed to have found evidence that the navigator 'John Cabot', an Italian who discovered North America in 1497, had received financial backing for his voyage from the Italian community in London at that time.

COMMENCING WORK IN LONDON

After his temporary summer job in Polperro, Cornwall, Santo came to London in September 1960 to seek work through an agency and he initially found a position at Brusa's in St Martin's Lane where he stayed for six months. This was an Italian restaurant next door to the Coliseum.

An advertisement for Brusa's appears in Tatler,
in December 1955. Image © Illustrated London News Group.
(*Image created courtesy of The British Library Board*)

Prior to this, in January 1953, a Mr Bickerstaff provided the first mention of pizza in a London restaurant in a 'Dining Out With I. Bickerstaff' column. The quote from this publication written by him was that; "Brusa's (in St. Martin's Lane, next to Coliseum), is the place where they make a speciality of the round, flat, savoury pastry that lowered Mr Eisenhower's reputation in Naples a month ago when he inadvertently said that he had eaten a better Pizza Napoletana in New York than in the Neapolitan capital. Also, that although Brusa's is usually rather crowded, it is highly Italian!"

A year later, attitudes towards pizza had changed even more. Mentioned in Tatler's society pages was that at a gathering of diplomats and minor royalty, the hostess had provided delicious Italian pizza at 'an informal supper party'. In London especially, this, along with the presidential gaffe, caused a rebound which meant that within a few months, pizza went from being "a baked sandwich, sweet or otherwise" to a Neapolitan speciality at Brusa's Fifty Restaurant in St Martin's Lane. Also on offer was Napoletana, prepared in a specially constructed oven to ensure that this popular dish was 'properly presented' as it is alleged it seldom was elsewhere at that time.

Two internal views of Brusa's Fifty Italian Restaurant.

(Disclaimer: every attempt to gain official permission from "Illustrated London News", at 46-48 East Smithfield London E1 1AW, for the use of this material has so far failed 6th July 2021).

Apparently, London's very first Italian Eating House was opened off Leicester Square by the Venetian Joseph Moretti between 1803 and 1805. Later, in 1856, the 'Illustrated Times' featured an Italian and French restaurant in Rupert Street owned by a Louis Stucchi. Neither of these seemed to have served pizza. It is assumed that pizza has existed for centuries and today's version from flatbreads appeared in the late eighteenth and early nineteenth centuries, sold from market stalls, especially in Naples. There is an interesting account of 'Olivellis' in Store Street, Bloomsbury, which had a chain of four and claimed to be the home of London's first pizza. A Sicilian restaurateur, Giovanni Salamone, bought Olivelli Bloomsbury in 1993, and, during the restoration work, discovered a large battered old shoebox containing photos of the Marx Brothers, Danny Kaye, Mae West,

Bob Hope, Mickey Rooney, Liberace and other stars of the 1930s and 40s, with messages of tribute to the owners, Rita and Enrico Olivelli.

This shoebox also contained a crumpled piece of paper on which was written the original restaurant's recipe for Pizza Margarita, as the first evidence of pizza in London. Sadly, it was later discovered to have been stolen by some customers who had been shown the contents of the box during their dining experience.

Brusa's address at 50 St Martin's Lane, was on the site of the present-day Côte Brasserie. Santo worked here for six months for £9 per week (£174 in today's terms) plus £2 tips and his hours were 11- 3 pm and 6 to 12 pm. Then a friend from the north of Sicily suggested a change of jobs and a wage increase to £12 per week. This was to be at 'Chez Solange,' a French restaurant at 35 Cranbourne Street where Santo worked for the same employer for four and a half years, this being the requirement to gain his work permit and the freedom to work anywhere in England, although, at that time, only in the catering industry.

La Cava and Le Chalet at Chez Solange, 35 Cranbourn Street, London WC2.

Chez Solange, which opened in 1959 and was apparently named after the son of Theresa and Rene Rochon, had three listed directors, four employees and gained a good reputation. The actor John Hurt, a frequent customer, recalled that it cost 17s 6d for three courses for two people (Evening Standard report). He still remembered the côte de porc and in his view, this was the best place for a nightcap.

The British Newspaper Archive quotes John Baker White's 'Good Eating Guide', mentioning the wisdom of booking a table. Rene Rochon,

Chef at Chez Solange near London's Leicester Square preparing his speciality dish of coq au vin and his wife Theresa, from Montargis near Orleans, who did quite a lot of their own cooking.

Theresa Rochon and Rene Rochon in December 1959.
(*Photos by Shutterstock*).

Dianne Nottle, 35 years a journalist and 20 as editor of the New York Times, coached international students and founded the English for Journalists blog on 3rd October 2010. She remembered Chez Solange, which made "the world's best chicken in cream sauce that had now sadly disappeared from Cranbourn Street". Other notable clients whom Santo remembered were Shirley Bassey and the Italian actress Claudia Cardinale.

On completing his four years, the Home Office sent Santo a letter stating that he could now do whatever he liked and go into any occupation he chose as he was now legally employed. In addition, from now on, having once started a job, he was to be asked why by the Home Office every time he wished to change to another position. He would usually tell them that he wanted to move from one job to another to work with people he knew from his home village, apart, of course, from making more money which had been the case with his transfer to Chez Solange. Several years later, his friend Alfonso would say, 'Santo, do you want to leave your present job as I have a possibility for you?' By now, Santo had worked in catering for a total of nearly five years, having enjoyed it despite the anti-social hours and a salary of £12 per week (£233 in today's terms). By contrast, a barber's shop pay would be less, say £9 per week, with perhaps small tips such as 6 pence or a shilling.

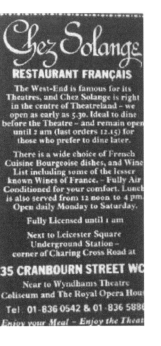

AT LAST - THE OPPORTUNITY FOR HAIRDRESSING IN LONDON!

Santo recalls, "As my wife and I now wanted to start a family and for me to have more sociable working hours and more leisure time, we were aware this would also mean having less income."

A Mr James, a Jewish gentleman who had a barber shop in Roehampton, was planning to open a second shop, at 16 Proctor Street, Holborn, London WC1. Here, Santo was to work for nearly twenty-five years, the earlier part of this time being with Alphonso Gambino from Ribera and a Giuseppe Campione. There was also a Giovanni, from the north of Sicily and they all knew one another well. However, when Alfonso returned home in 1964, Mr James asked Santo to take over as manager, a position he held until 1971, the year of Mr James' death. This business was known as 'Paul Stephen' and had really been named after his two sons, Paul and Stephen.

Paul Stephen in Proctor Street.

Paul Stephen from the opposite side of Proctor Street, Holborn.

Inside the salon.

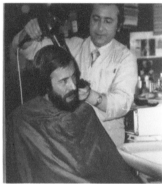
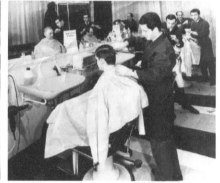

With some of the staff inside the salon.

A client from the Paul Stephen years, Tony Shepherd, first met Santo at Proctor Street in 1972 when he was working in Red Lion Square, looking for a hairdresser, and in his words, 'There he was'. He often had to wait two hours to be seen because it was so busy, but he liked the way Santo cut his hair, which he still had in those days, and did him a line-up with clippers.

He also liked the atmosphere and vibe of the salon which was very convenient for his workplace and the customers and staff at the Proctor

Street salon. There were perhaps four or five Italian staff who liked football and were very amiable. In those days, a haircut was usually a 'short back and sides', until you were about sixteen when you sought something better with more self-expression and style. Tony came in once a week, every Tuesday at 8 am, not regarding it as a barber's, but a hair stylist's. At this time, the Beatles were setting a hairstyle trend of their own, as were other pop stars. When Tony's work base changed to Euston and later to Borough High Street, he used to get to Santo early before work, sometimes arriving on his doorstep before the salon opened. Tony went on to work for two years in South Africa and would return to England for six weeks in the summer and six weeks in the winter. He liked the fact that Santo paid more attention to detail and cutting with the scissors. Even up to Tony's sudden death in 2020, Santo did him a line-up when he shaved his head, which, incidentally, most hairdressers don't do. Finding a hairdresser to do this whilst Tony was in South Africa was no easy task.

A line-up seems to have its origins with Afro-Caribbean hairstyles and can be a work of art. It involves creating an abrupt hairline cut with clippers at the side, at the edge of the hairline, plus designs at the side to make a 'trendy hairdo'.

Tony Shepherd, left, as best man at a friend's wedding.

When Santo moved to Chichester Rents, Tony found himself in the company of 'legal eagles', one who used to talk about rugby at length as he was on the disciplinary panel for the Rugby Union. Tony was, by now, a big Chelsea football fan and had an annual season ticket. He found personalities from the Inns of Court particularly interesting as well as several celebrities who now frequented the salon.

Santo's son, Jack, who now manages the business, remembered Lord Denning and snooker personalities such as Steve Davis. As to Tony Shepherd's views on the future for hairdressing in the city of London, there is a problem of ever-increasing rents which means you have to be in or part of a large organisation in order to survive. Up to his recent death in 2020, Tony lived in Clapham where there was a shop run by hairdressers from Kurdistan. They would offer rates undercutting the established local hairdressers. From his experience in South Africa, he had learned that shops there could operate rent-free for around two years to encourage the development of a new business, but here, they don't seem to want to do this. Illustrating escalating changes in personal living expenses, Tony used to take all his clothes to the dry cleaners when he was working full time. However, this had now become too expensive so he reverted to using his own washing machine.

Another of Santo's very regular clients was one Giovanni Bertelli who worked at the Hilton Park Lane and came three times a week for a hair-trim and shampoo. He was eventually to successfully run a nightclub in Berkeley Square, but he sadly died at a young age. There were also some judges and lawyers from Chichester Rents, Chancery Lane, such as Judge George with whom Santo's son Jack had long conversations as he always liked a chat. Santo was actually invited by Judge George's wife to attend his funeral. He was a busy person and Santo recalled being asked for an 'early appointment' at 7.30 in the morning, which meant an even earlier car drive to work from his home in Southgate! Santo further recalled that 'some of the judges followed us for their hairstyling when we transferred from Chichester Rents to St Paul's Square, and others even to our present site near Woodside College Bounds Green'. Some have even sought time slots outside the official shop hours which demonstrates long-term customer loyalty, thereby giving much personal satisfaction to both Santo and his son Jack.

Figaro at Chichester Rents. (*Courtesy of the Local Data Company*)

Staff and a client at Proctor Street.

THE ELEMENTS
FOR BUSINESS SUCCESS

Over a period of fifty-five years, Santo Raia established himself as a barber of the 'scissor-cut style for a reasonable fee', for both men and women. Now at the age of 82, he still owns a salon called 'Figaro' with his son Jack, who currently manages this establishment near Woodside College, Bounds Green, Friern Barnet in North London. The author first met Santo in the early 1970s at his salon at 16 Proctor Street, Holborn WC1, where Santo had posted pictures of models' profiles on the wall to assist clients in choosing a style or cut beyond mere hair maintenance. At that time, this writer had a dread of being 'scalped', something that he and his peers had become accustomed to from adolescence. Santo was to engender confidence that there was an alternative. This would lead to an association and a friendship over many years and is why this short work has now come to be written about a barber 'with a real difference'.

We have already referred to the input of family members as one of the characteristics of Italian business and Ellie Raia, who would eventually become Santo's daughter-in-law after marrying his son Jack, recalled that she started working in Holborn in 1990 on leaving school. In her words:

"I had always known what I wanted to do with my life, and it was hairdressing, although there had been other options. My uncle found me a job at Hair Design in Proctor Street on the opposite side to Paul Stephen and I started working as a junior, which involved washing clients' hair and making teas and coffees. Santo would come in every so often to say hello and I took to him straight away because he was so loving and treated me like a daughter.

Ellie Raia

I would sometimes return his visit at Paul Stephen. After a few years and attending college part-time, I passed the City and Guilds Certificate in Hairdressing and then began to cut hair myself. I remember going to Santo on one occasion and he said, 'Quickly, cut my sideburns for me!' We'd have a laugh and a chat and I would run back to my work afterwards. I so enjoyed going to see him and he became like a father figure to me.

Eventually, the hairdressers' I worked for moved to other premises and I carried on working with them for a further year or so, then went to work closer to home. Six months passed before I would meet Santo again and he told me that he was moving to Chichester Rents in Chancery Lane and that if ever I wanted a job, I could have one there.

Consequently, in June 2000, I went to work with him and Jack at Figaro's in Chichester Rents. Although hairdressing was all I had actually known, I found that barbering had a different set of skills and techniques which Santo, and later Jack, would teach me."

Barbering is really about beard trimming, shaving and the management of short hair and is confined to the needs of men. The most famous barber in history is purported to be Ambrose Pare (1510-1590) at a time when barbers not only cut hair but sometimes performed gruesome and painful surgery. By contrast, a hairdresser was a person who cut and shaped hair. Ellie continues: "I was also to learn a great deal from observing others performing their art. Although I have been in this business now for thirty-one years, I can honestly say that you can learn something new every day." (This phrase is reiterated in the introduction of this book, that in hairdressing, there is always something new to learn).

Continuous Uncertainty for Business Strategy

Over the past twenty years or so, there have been so many changes. Santo is now officially retired and Jack continues to run the business alone. Through the uncertainty and frustration, common in any precarious profession, being compounded by perpetual tenancy terminations and a reduction in the availability of small business premises in Central London at reasonably affordable rents, they, like many others, have been the victims of the activities of developers, property speculators and overseas investors in or near the City of London. Prior to arriving in Friern Barnet, they left a successful location in Chichester Rents, off Drury Lane, after seventeen years with only one year's notice. This was followed by nomadic prospecting and after a chance meeting with a Turkish contact, they were able to rent chairs in an existing hairdressing business at St Paul's Square, Ludgate Hill, for about a year, until this too was to have its lease terminated, resulting in a move to outer London. Although no longer in Central London, this is a more secure operation which Jack admits he has now grown to prefer as it is more dependable. This is especially true since he has only recently learnt that the chair he rents on a Monday at a city hairdresser's will no longer be available due to the termination of that business lease as well. Consequently, this is a situation with which he has become all too familiar and it remains to be seen whether post-lockdown, this over-speculation on property, as well as increasing rateable values, will come to a halt for several years, especially if a recession sets in.

Unusual Customer Demands and Situations

Jack recalls some unusual situations and quite a few embarrassing moments, when one of his father's regulars, who he had served for years, would return every month and ask for the salon radio to be switched off. If this was not done, he would 'get the hump' and become quite rude. "My father had done his hair for years but he was never able to tell us his name and he would only answer to "Sir". There was another chap whom we regarded as a friend over some forty years. On one occasion, after having a haircut, he told us that he had forgotten his wallet and would be back to pay. We never in a million years thought that not only would he not return, but we would never see him again!" This was very strange and requires an acknowledgement of the idiosyncrasies of people in a service industry.

There was an Arab client whom Jack considered to have had a long-standing and close relationship with his father. He possessed a Cartier lighter, probably valued at £650, and he asked Jack to go to a shop and buy some matches. By the time Jack had returned, he had given this lighter to his father Santo as a gift. What would one make of that?

On another occasion, two regular customers came in one day, announcing themselves as VAT inspectors and asked to see the books to check that all was in order. Fortunately, this information could be provided through the business audit. Perhaps one must always expect the unpredictable in a people industry.

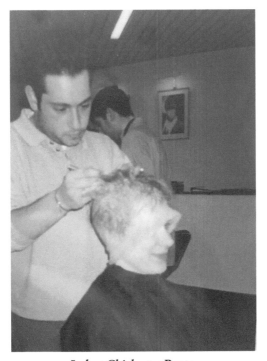

Jack at Chichester Rents.

HAIR CUTTING METHODS OVER FIFTY YEARS

The salon in Friern Barnet.

Hairstyling today is big business and way beyond the aspirations of fifty years ago when all that was on offer was 'A Short Back and Sides' or a 'Boston Back', where the hair was trimmed in a straight line at the back of the neck for a few pounds. This was done through the 'Clippers Route' producing a 'tidy' haircut, by means of an electric, or previously manual, styling tool to trim the hair to a uniform length on the hairline. Very short hair was the requirement, especially in the serving forces, in the interests of easy maintenance and hygiene. A guard was placed in front of the blade to protect the scalp and ensure the hair was within the cutting edges. Blades were adjusted for different hair lengths such as 1 - 3.4mm, 2 - 6.4mm, 3 - 9.5mm, 4 - 12.7mm, 7 - 22.2mm and 8 - 25.4mm. By contrast, it is scissors with different blade types that are used by barbers and stylists to manually and more precisely thin and trim the hair, taking longer but allowing for a greater variety of lengths, textures and finished styles.

Today, both men and women might seek to follow the hairstyles of celebrities even at prices of £50 and upwards per session. Nowadays, the dictates of fleeting fashion and increased affluence have resulted in more men and women being prepared to pay higher prices which means longer appointment times. Styles are continually changing, especially for the young and impressionable, determined by their role models, including film stars.

The nature of some work has also changed, raising the fundamental issue that, if new corporate offices blocks have been created to accommodate more employees, when and where do their staff go for their hairdressing? During flexible lunchtimes or after work, perhaps? Will there be as many employees seeking haircuts? The recent lockdowns have forced some major changes, such as a future when more employees might be working from home for several days a week, or be self-employed or perhaps be offered 'just in time' or 'ad hoc' contracts or services. In such cases, when and where will these clients fit in their coiffure? Will they seek home visits? For those in direct personal contact with customers in service industries, such as hotels and restaurants, there currently is a requirement for face-to-face customer interaction, perhaps less business formality, but still a need for personal appearance and interactive skills which demonstrate competence to garner customer confidence in the service provider.

All this begs the question of what implications these issues might have for the future of hairdressing. Although the coronavirus pandemic has had a major impact on the profession, some online sources might reveal different influences for particular customer markets. For instance, the view of Mark Maciver, aka 'SliderCuts', is that gaining a reputation is done through giving good haircuts and receiving personal recommendations which is the tried and tested form of marketing, but more than this, his customer base grew further when the internet developed and then social media came along, which enabled his reputation to spread faster and wider. Now he has customers from all over London and even some from overseas.

This means perhaps creating attractive content and a lively social media presence on platforms such as Facebook, Twitter and Instagram. Complementing this must be the provision to niche markets of a consistently good, professional service which is efficient, reliable and trustworthy as well as having comprehensive website facilities with an emphasis on marketing and personal recommendations from existing clients. This might mean perhaps having a particular affinity with a specific community or customer base, just as Santo had in Proctor Street and Chichester Rents with rugby enthusiasts as well as legal professionals. All of this requires taking an interest in clients and their business and produces a sure foundation to encourage and set up networks and customer loyalty programmes.

Jack Raia at the North London salon.

Jack would not predict a secure future for hairdressing in Central London due to the continuous increases in both rent and rates, already mentioned, that are especially challenging for small businesses and which Jack states are unjustifiable. He feels that these expenses alone are prohibitive and make meeting all the other business costs impossible.

When renting a chair, Jack has to pay all his own expenses for any products he uses, for the maintenance of his equipment and for parking his car. A cut and blow-dry costs from £50+ to £80 and for colours, depending on the procedure, from £100 to £200. It is unlikely to yield much in the way of profit other than to maintain long-standing relationships. On a personal level, he still likes going to his city base on a Monday because it gives him a change of scene and enables him to keep in touch with some of his old clients.

It is still possible for him to do this, providing he can cover his expenses. although it might not guarantee profitability in the longer term.

Another factor is that to practice as a barber in this country, you don't have to have a qualification or a 'certificate of competence', whereas, on the continent, local authority inspectors monitor businesses on these issues. Jack took a hairdressing qualification at level three at a local college and because he had previous salon experience, he condensed it into six months before receiving accreditation.

Haircare services could include trichological and maintenance packages, which is an avenue Jack would currently not venture down since special qualifications are needed and extensive resources required. Perhaps even basic maintenance of a healthy scalp through taking samples for microscopic observation would be over-ambitious, since it would require laboratory facilities and qualified hair specialists such as those at the well-established Belgravia Centre Trichology Group in London's Victoria and Liverpool Street.

Some barbers might claim to offer part of this service which is questionable. Jack has customers who have been for hair restorative procedures in other countries such as Turkey for say £2,500 for each year, whereas in the UK, this might be £7,500. Topically, there are environmental issues such as the conservation of water and the colours used as well as technologies, advocated by some hairdressers, who might be offering them without having any formal qualifications. The question is how do they acquire this knowledge? Perhaps it comes from working in a salon where there is a hairdresser who has this expertise from whom they glean as much information as possible by observing their procedures. Perhaps a hairdresser has learnt techniques from watching videos on YouTube from which they claim to know the subject. As there are no business inspections to monitor these 'professional' methods in this country, they are open to exploitation by the unscrupulous. If your profession or training in your home country has not been regulated, should you seek to set up in another? You may require proof that you have practised your profession for at least one year during the last decade.

Then there is unfair competition when perhaps an immigrant opens a shop situated near to an existing business and undercuts it by undercharging and working at volume. "We have one currently near to us who was actually photographed working at 2.30 in the morning!" says Jack. In order to survive, existing businesses have to meet their expenses and therefore cannot operate in a climate of undercutting, otherwise, eventually, they have to close down if their clientele is severely reduced.

Taking all this into account, Jack would not encourage any of his three sons to follow him into this business. However, perusing through information online about the future of barbering suggests a more upbeat perception that the demand for it was increasing prior to the recent lockdowns.

The second location of Santo and Jack's hairdressing business at Chichester Rents was, according to the Local Data Company, a modern redevelopment of the original alley and previous buildings along Chancery Lane. It has an interesting history in that the passage itself was named after the Bishops of Chichester who had a mansion off Chancery Lane on the Lincoln's Inn site and which became the possession of a Ralph Neville, a Bishop and Chancellor in the 13th century. The area adjoining Chancery Lane was largely built up by the mid-16th century and Ogilby and Morgan's map of 1676 seems to show the first tentative outlines of the alleys in this part of town. It seems to have been a wide-open space with lots of narrow tall buildings, largely rebuilt in Georgian times but retaining the alley as an open space. In the latter part of the 19th century, some of the buildings were redeveloped as single blocks, the façades being retained as part of a 1980's redevelopment. In the 1970s and 1980s, there was an open alleyway that was lined with modest shops, eateries and a public house until 1989.

In 2012, a planning application was made that would see the 1980's façades removed and a new modern design introduced with dramatic staggered walkways. It almost saw Chichester Rents vanish entirely, but eventually, it was agreed that the rebuilding of the surrounding offices should include retention of the alleyway. The redevelopment of that office block has, however, created the very modern appearance of this ancient thoroughfare. The overbridge is a clever design, as it is narrowest and most "bridge-like" at the bottom, but by the time you get to the top floor, it becomes so wide that it is easy to forget it is a bridge at all, and not just part of an open-plan office. The saddest factor for Santo and Jack was that for them, a new business here has now become too expensive for them to operate.

Star Yard entrance.

The view from Chancery Lane

Santo and Marianna celebrating their Golden Wedding

THE UNIQUENESS OF
THE ISLAND OF SICILY

Although it was not the original intention of this biography to include a detailed account of the long and fascinating history of Sicily, there is much that makes this island exceptional. It is the largest in the Mediterranean, has some striking features and also a unique past. A more comprehensive view of its qualities and culture could, therefore, provide a deeper understanding of the potential any Sicilian such as Santo and his associates might have to contribute to any destination they may migrate to. This is in addition to the reasons for Italian immigration to 'Little Italy' in Clerkenwell, London and also to New York, as discussed earlier.

The historian Professor Michael Scott has recently featured in an extremely well-researched and superbly presented series of programmes for the BBC. There is also an excellent book by Jeremy Dummett entitled, 'Syracuse: City of Legends', published by Tauris Parke of Bloomsbury Publishing, which has been used as a source in this section. Also referenced as background to this biography is 'Sicily, A Short History from the Ancient Greeks to Cosa Nostra', by John Julius Norwich, published in 2015 by John Murray Publishers, which is masterfully entertaining, comprehensive and excellently researched.

Firstly, John Julius Norwich states that Italy has a plethora of traditions and customs, whereas Sicily has had a few differences which set it apart from those on the mainland. He quotes the statements of Goethe, that "Sicily is the key to everything." First of all, the largest island in the Mediterranean, although it has proved over the centuries to be the most unhappy, Sicily is a steppingstone between Europe and Africa and the gateway between the East and the West as well as a link between the Latin world and the Greek.

It previously functioned as a stronghold, a clearing house, and an observation point and was fought over and occupied in turn by all the great powers which had striven over the centuries to extend their domination over the Middle Sea. More significantly is that it has belonged to them all but has probably been part of none. Again, in the words of John Julius Norwich, "Today, despite the beauty of its landscape and the fertility of its fields, there lingers a dark brooding quality of opportunities lost and promises unfulfilled." More crucially important now is that Sicily is less unhappy than it has been for centuries since it became a part of Italy itself.

However, the traditional mafia is still operating, having a role in local government, real estate, and other dealings in certain communities. Still ingrained in Sicily are the traditional religious festivals that occur in cities and families remain incredibly close-knit.

The Sicilian people as a whole are very laid back and relaxed; in most areas, shops and restaurants are closed between 1 pm and 4 pm most weekdays for long lunches, as people dine and spend time with one another during a siesta period.

Whereas the Italian language is almost entirely Latin-based, Sicilian has elements of Greek, Arabic, French, Catalan and Spanish. Highly significant is that a great deal of Italian influence has only occurred since 1860, following unification. Questioning the reasons for this idyllic island being different from the mainland, John Julius Norwich concludes that it is the result of a multiplex of invaders, interlopers and wanderers who have contributed to Sicily's varied architecture and education. The Sicilian language isn't commonly used today except perhaps in remote villages, although it is still mixed with formal Italian in the larger cities. Unlike Italian, it sounds more like a blend of Spanish and French and it is said that most Italians find it hard to understand. Sicily's multicultural history is displayed in its architecture and cuisine and evidence of ancient civilisations can be viewed by visiting caves and grottos and observing cave paintings in the North West. It is believed that the first inhabitants arrived in 5000 BC and were the Sicani from North Africa, the Siculi from the Italian continent and the Elymi from Greece. In 900 BC, these were succeeded by the Phoenicians who founded the ancient city of Carthage in North Africa and Palermo in Sicily.

Ancient Burials in Sicily (*Courtesy of Shutterstock*)

Sicily's fertile landscapes and its abundance of natural produce such as olives and vines, captured the attention of the Ancient Greeks arriving in Naxos, around 750 BC. Eager to take advantage of the profitable trading opportunities this bountiful island offered, the Greeks colonised it along with much of southern Italy, dubbing the region Magna Graecia or Greater Greece.

TEMPLE AT AGRIGENTO

The remnants of Ancient Greece are a fundamental attraction of modern Sicily today, with world-class archaeological sites at Agrigento, Segesta, Selinunte and Eraclea Minoa. This was a period of the island's history when bitter conflicts waged between Greek settlements and the Carthaginians, who originated from the ancient Phoenician city-state and civilization founded around 814 BC and located in present-day Tunisia. The battle of Himera with Greece in 450 BC, which defeated the Carthaginians, was the cause of one turning point in the history of the island and three Punic Wars between Carthage and Rome, fought between 264 and 146, were another. Conflict between the Carthaginians and Rome was to resume at a later stage until Sicily was finally brought under Roman power for 500 years allowing it to prosper and become a 'Granary of Rome'. It would be corruption, the rise of the Emperor Constantine's influence and the rise of Christianity that would lead to the decline of the Roman Empire.

Part of the damaged colossal marble statue of the Emperor Constantine the Great. (*Courtesy of Google Unsplash*)

Sicily was invaded and fought over by the Vandals from North Africa and the Ostrogoths (a 5th-century Roman-era Germanic people who settled in the Balkans) and the Byzantines, (the Eastern Roman Empire whose capital was Constantinople). Then, in the 9th century, the Arabs, the Berbers (Moroccans, Libyans, Tunisians) and the Spanish Muslims, known as Saracens, would then become the rulers of Sicily. Roman inheritance can still be viewed to the present day at the Villa Romana del Casale, a large and elaborate Roman villa or palace located about 3 km from the town of Piazza Armerina. Excavations have revealed this to be one of the richest, largest, and most varied collections of Roman mosaics in the world. As a result, it has been designated a UNESCO World Heritage Site and demonstrates the luxurious lifestyles favoured by the Romans.

A Preserved Mosaic Floor from the Villa.

The villa and artwork date back to the early 4th century AD. The mosaic floors cover some 3,500 sq metres and are almost unique in their excellent state of preservation thanks to landslides and floods which covered the remains. Although less well-known, there is an extraordinary collection of frescoes that covered not only the interior rooms but also the exterior walls. Again, according to the historian John Julius Norwich, in the 9th century, Sicily began to recognise its potential. The Arabs, the Berbers and the Saracens had conquered and ruled the island and also cultivated the land, introducing some sophisticated systems of irrigation and prize produce like oranges and lemons. In addition to this, there was Arabian art, literature and mathematics. They designated Palermo as the 'Emirate of Sicily' and eventually it would have 100 mosques.

At this time, the economy thrived and all enjoyed a period of religious tolerance, explaining the attraction of Sicily for Europeans who wished to capitalise upon it.

THE NORMAN INVASION OF SOUTHERN SICILY

King Roger 11 of Sicily Crowned by Jesus Christ (*Courtesy of Shutterstock*)

The diverse and tolerant culture bred by King Roger resulted in an incredible blend of architectural style with a fusion of Arabian and Byzantine features eventually to be defined as 'Sicilian Romanesque'. Here was a unique style of art and architecture that can be seen in the churches and cathedrals of Palermo. Examples of this are the Palazzo dei Normanni (Norman Palace), the Capella Palatina (Palatine Chapel) and a magnificent castle at Erice.

The Normans enjoyed a lavish lifestyle and King Roger commissioned many palaces and monuments to be built. Palermo thrived under Norman rule and became the wealthiest hub in Sicily. *(This file is licensed under the Creative Commons Attribution-Share Alike 4.0 International license.) Also, Shutterstock.*

Views of the Palatine Chapel in the Norman Palace

For many people, this is the superlative portrait of Christ in all Christian Art

However, this opulent period was not to last, and, after merely a century, the Norman dynasty came to an end, succeeded in 1194 by Friedrich II and the more modest Swabian Hohenstaufen or southern Germans, followed by a succession of other rulers.

The French.

Sicily fell to Charles I, Duke of Anjou (modern-day Western France), in 1250. He ruled until 1282 when King Peter 111 of Aragon (Spain) successfully invaded. He was followed by other relatives keeping the island as a part of the crown of Aragon until 1409. There were several revolutions with the decline of the Normans, and, despite religious tolerance, there were conflicts between Christians and Muslims. Sicily fell in succession back to the French, then to the Spanish and then to Austrian rule before the Spanish Bourbons united the island with Naples in 1734.

The Spanish.

Under Bourbon rule, it was lost due to a revolution, but regained again in 1860 when Giuseppe Garibaldi, an Italian general, patriot and republican, marched with his army of irregular troops to unite Sicily with the other Italian regions and create what is known today as 'The Kingdom of Italy'. However, in 1866, Palermo rebelled against Italy, the city was bombed and Italian soldiers were summarily executed. In the aftermath, rebels took over the island, resulting in poverty, and between 1871 and 1914, prior to the start of World War 1 a large number of Sicilians emigrated to the United States. A powerful separatist movement fought for Sicily to be admitted as a US state (it would have been the 49th state, preceding Alaska and Hawaii). However, as an appeasement, the Italian government awarded Sicily special status, and from 1946 to this day, it has been declared an autonomous region of Italy.

The Allies' quest for power in Sicily included approaching the Mafia for assistance and supporting their criminal network. Mafioso Don Calogero Vizzini was a key figure and the Sicilian Mafia became a frightening political force for 50 years. A large heroin and cocaine trafficking network was established from Palermo to New York and criminal lifestyles became the inspiration for many major Hollywood films. This situation lasted until the 1990s when a number of major criminals were prosecuted in highly publicised trials.

A WORLD HERITAGE SITE

Among Sicily's historic sites is the Valley of Greek temples in Agrigento, the oldest town in Sicily, with many ancient ruins and some amazing architecture.

Temple of Concordia

From inside the ruined temple

Thanks to its good state of preservation, the Temple of Concordia is ranked amongst the most notable buildings of the Greek civilization that exists today. The UNESCO listing cites the temple's six-Doric-column facade. There were 6 x 13 columns built over a basement of 39.44 x 16.9m2 and each Doric column has twenty grooves. The upper frame had gutters with lion-like protomes (the head and torso of an animal or human) and the roof was covered with marble tiles. When the temple was turned into a church, the entrance was moved to the rear, the rear wall of the cellar being destroyed. The spaces between the columns were closed, while 12 arched openings were created in the cellar to produce a structure with one nave and two aisles and the pagan altar was destroyed. (All these pictures are by courtesy of Creative Commons).

TEMPLE OF HERA LACINIA

Built about 450 BC, it is also known as Temple D and is the sister temple to Concordia. Hera was the Olympian queen of the gods and goddess of women. She was the wife of Zeus.

Temple D Sister Temple to Concordia (*Courtesy of Creative Commons*)

There is evidence of a fire following the siege of Akragas in 406 BC. This temple was restored during the Roman occupation and the terracotta roof was replaced with one of marble, having a steeply inclined slope on the Eastern side. The original temple was dedicated to the Greek goddess Hera Lacinia, and, after Roman restoration, to the goddess Juno Lacinia.

Selinunte was an ancient Greek city on the South West coast of Sicily, situated between the valleys of the Cottone and Modione rivers. It now lies in the *comune* Castelvetrano, between Triscina di Selinunte in the west and Marinella di Selinunte in the east. This archaeological site originally contained five temples centred on an acropolis. Of the five temples, only The Temple of Hera Lacinia or Juno Lacinia, otherwise known as Temple D, remains.

The Valle dei Templi, where stands the building also known as "Temple E", is a section of the ancient city of Agrigentum (ancient Greek Akragas, modern Agrigento) in *Sicily* which has been re-erected. At its peak before 409 BC, the city may have contained up to 30,000 people, excluding slaves.

Temple E (*Courtesy of Creative Commons*)

The **Teatro Massimo Vittorio Emanuele** Opera House on the Piazza Verdi in Palermo was dedicated to King Victor Emanuel II. Noted for its perfect acoustics, it is the biggest in Italy and at the time of its inauguration, was the third largest opera house in Europe, after the Palais Garnier in Paris and the K.K Hof-Opernhaus in Vienna, Austria. After the unification of Italy in 1861, Filippo and Ernesto Basile spent 20 years building this architectural masterpiece in the classic style, using local stone and marble. Its location marks the point where the ancient quarters and the new expanding city meet.

Teatro Massimo Vittorio Emanuele Opera House (*Courtesy of Shutterstock*)

The Auditorium of the opera house (*Courtesy of Shutterstock*)

The cathedral Church at Palermo

The cathedral church of the Roman Catholic Archdiocese of Palermo is dedicated to the Assumption of the Virgin Mary. The different styles of architecture are due to a long history of additions, alterations and restorations. It was erected in 1185 by Walter Ophamil (a.k.a. Gualtiero Offamiglio and Walter of the Mill), Dean of Agrigento, and Archbishop of Palermo 1168–1191. He was also "Il Primo Ministro" – The first minister of the crown and the Anglo-Norman Archbishop of Palermo and King William II's minister. This cathedral, created in the 12th century, is of Arab and Norman architecture. Additions and renovations integrated Gothic, Baroque and Neo-Classical design.

Inside the Cathedral (*By courtesy of Alamy*)

The jewel-studded Byzantine crown of Constance of Aragon, who was the wife of Frederick 11, can also be seen here. The reconstruction of this cathedral took place early in the 18th century after the crushing earthquake of 1693. As a part of UNESCO World Heritage Sites in Italy, it is considered an excellent example of Baroque architecture.

St Nicholas on Noto (*Courtesy of Getty Images*)

This cathedral, built in the 12th century, is a combination of both Arab and Norman architecture, with additions and renovations incorporated in Gothic, Baroque and Neo-Classical styles. Reconstruction of the cathedral took place in the early 18th century following a devastating earthquake in 1693. This building is considered a towering example of Baroque art among the many UNESCO World Heritage Sites in Italy.

Modica

During the 20th century, the city was extended with the development of the new suburbs, Sacro Cuore (or "Sorda") and Monserrato Idria, which are often referred to as Modern Modica. The old and modern quarters of the city are connected by one of Europe's highest bridges, the Guerrieri bridge, 120 metres (394ft) high and 300 metres (980ft) long.

Despite the earthquakes of 1613 and 1693, and floods of 1833 and 1902, Modica has retained some of the most beautiful architecture in Sicily. Much of it was rebuilt after the 1693 earthquake with imposing and conspicuous urban monuments in the Sicilian Baroque style. As with many other parts of the city, the large Baroque Cathedral of "San Giorgio", dedicated to St George, dates back to the Middle Ages and the front of the Cathedral has a staircase of 300 steps leading down to lower Modica, or 'Modica Bassa'.

The Duomo San Giorgio ('Dome of St. George'), located in Modica, in the Province of Ragusa is the Mother Church of the city and is also classified as a UNESCO World Heritage Site. The building is the final result of the 18th-century reconstruction, which took place following the disastrous earthquakes that struck Modica in 1542, 1613 and also in 1693. Reconstruction work commenced in 1702 and finished in 1738. Further works were carried out, culminating in the affixing of the iron cross to the spire in 1842 and this marked the definitive appearance of the church. According to the art historian Maurizio Fagiolo dell'Arco, the Church should be included among "the seven wonders of the baroque world".

Duomo San Georgio in Modica, Sicily (*Courtesy of Shutterstock*)

Outstanding Sights

The Neapolis Archaeological Park is a natural area full of archaeological finds, belonging to several eras of Syracusan history. Because of the quantity and grandeur of its monuments, it is regarded as one of the most important archaeological areas in Sicily and the largest in the Mediterranean.

Only five minutes walk from the Greek Theatre of Syracuse is the Orecchio di Dionisio, a limestone cave carved out of the Temenites Hill, over 100 feet tall and shaped like an ear. It was given its name by the painter Michelangelo da Caravaggio. The marvellous acoustics of the cave mean that what you whisper at one end is audible everywhere. This is the legendary prison of the tyrant Dionysius.

The Ear of Dionysius (*Courtesy of Alamy*)

Magnificent Greek and Roman Theatres

The Greek Theatre of Taormina is the most enthralling historical monument of the Ionian Sea, that part of the Mediterranean lying between Albania (to the North East), Greece (to the East), Sicily (to the South West), and Italy (to the West and North West). It was regarded by ancient authors as a section of the Adriatic Sea, but it is now recognised as the Ionian Sea and a separate body of water. As one of the world's most popular tourist attractions, it was noted by **Johann Wolfgang Goethe** in his famous "Journey to Italy" where he writes, "*No theatre audience has ever had such a sight in front.*" This is the second-largest Greek theatre, after Syracuse, with a view of Mount Etna in the foreground.

The Theatre at Taormina (Courtesy of Shutterstock)

Historic Theatres which Still Survive and Give Performances to this Day

Created to accommodate dramatic performances or musical events, this Greek-Roman theatre is divided into three parts: the **scene**, the **orchestra** and the **auditorium**. The stage in front of the auditorium is the place where the actors played, and, according to the experts, during Roman reconstruction, this part was decorated with two rows of columns, one on top of the other. The stage also has three large arched openings, symmetrically distanced from each other, and six niches, three to the right and three to the left of the central arch. On the stage are the remains of six column bases and four Corinthian columns that were raised after 1860.

Ariel view of the Theatre at Syracuse (Courtesy of Wikipedia)

The Theatre of Syracuse lies on the south slopes of the Temenites Hill and overlooks the modern city of Syracuse in South-Eastern Sicily. It was first built in the 5th century BC, rebuilt in the 3rd century BC and renovated again in the Roman period. Consequently, Syracuse was the ancient capital. Almost every Greek city had a theatre because plays were part of many religious festivals and the Greeks enjoyed singing and dancing. At first, theatres were only used for festivals, built in the open air on hillsides and could often hold more than 18,000 spectators. In the late Imperial Roman period, the theatre was adapted for gladiatorial games, and later, with the fall of the Western Empire, it fell into disuse and the marble, as well as the monumental columns, were removed. Only after the end of the Second World War were some sections of the original construction completed through a major programme of restoration work. *(Notes from Wikipedia)*

SOME AUTHENTIC SICILIAN CUISINE AND WINES

Having reflected on some of the notable historical aspects of this island of Santo's birth, his biography would not be complete without some reference to its authentic cuisine. This is something in which Santo himself has taken much interest throughout his life, relishing cooking and entertaining family and friends at home. He has now been followed by two of his granddaughters, Cinzia and Rossario Roselli, who researched and supplied some of the recipes that now follow.

Surprisingly, and unlike that of the Italian Peninsula, the Sicilian diet is focused on grains, vegetables and fish. Although meat and game are available, they are used mainly for occasional and special dishes, rather than for everyday meals. Although its cuisine has similarities with the Italian Peninsula, Sicilian food has been influenced throughout its history by invaders such as the Greeks, the Spanish, the French and the Arabs, producing unique differences to add to its unique culture. The Arab influence of the 10th century brought in apricots, sugar, citrus fruits, melons, rice, saffron, raisins, nutmeg, cloves, pepper, pine nuts and cinnamon, and, on the Western corner of the island, couscous. The Normans were fond of meat and the Jews introduced garlic fried in olive oil into their sauces. The Spanish later introduced cocoa, maize, peppers, turkey and tomatoes from the New World. The Greeks had a preference for fish such as tuna, sea bream, sea bass, cuttlefish and swordfish and also introduced olives, pistachios and fresh vegetables such as broad beans and aubergine.

Sicilians today are recognised for seafood such as tuna and swordfish that are this island's staples. However, they are also well known for pasta and pizza, together with their lunchtime delicacy, the 'arancino' which is a fried rice croquette filled with a variety of meats and vegetables in a mix. They also coined the creation of cannolis, and are well-known for their delicious granita dessert. As opposed to incorporating the more expensive beef option for protein in dishes, they often use lamb or pork, and even horse, which may seem unusual but is an incredibly popular ingredient throughout Sicily.

Pasta-Rigatoni and Penne

Ingredients and Method:
This is included first as it is one of Santo's favourite dishes.

Prepare a Bechamel sauce until smooth with a blond roux and milk, then add tomato sauce and mozzarella cheese. Place the pre-boiled rigatoni and penne in an oven-proof dish. Add shark fish with slivers of sautéed onion and then pour over the sauce blended with black olives, vinegar and a pinch of sugar. Place into the oven and cook to a golden colour and serve with roasted potatoes.

Sarde a Beccafino

Sardines stuffed with raisins, pine nuts and breadcrumbs baked to a golden colour (*All Sources Wikipedia*)

Pasta alla Norma

Most Pasta alla Norma recipes consist of fried aubergines. The exception here is that they are roasted. Aubergine really absorbs oil like a sponge and roasting makes this recipe easier and less messy to prepare.

Stigghiole - spiced and grilled intestine from lamb or goat cooked in the oven.

Caponata

Roast the aubergine which has been cut into 1-inch cubes and seasoned with salt. Allow the salted cubes to sit in a colander for about an hour to sweat out any bitterness, but this is optional. Toss the aubergine with a generous amount of extra virgin olive oil and spread it out in a large pan. Roast in a pre-heated oven at 400 degrees F for about 25 to 30 minutes or until fully cooked and tender.

Separately, prepare some finely chopped onions, bell peppers and celery and cook in a skillet until soft in texture. Then add crushed tomatoes, capers, olives, raisins, honey, bay leaf and crushed pepper flakes. Stir in the vinegar and white wine. Add to the previously cooked aubergine and simmer on medium-low heat for 10 minutes. This dish is noted for its tangy flavour.

Arancini

Arancini are Italian rice balls made with a white wine risotto that is cooled and formulated into rounds or pear shapes, each containing a ball of minced meat or vegetables and a small round of mozzarella cheese. The shapes are immersed in egg-wash then breadcrumbs and deep-fried until golden brown.

The result is a gooey mozzarella centre. These are the island's specialities and are fantastic for lunch or dinner and can also be frozen for later cooking.

POPULAR SWEET DISHES

Sicilian Pignolata or fried honey balls.

Pignolata is a Sicilian pastry dessert which originated in Messina and is also common in Calabria. It is a soft pastry, covered in chocolate and lemon-flavoured syrup or icing. This pastry is half covered or iced in one flavour and the other half in the other flavour. Once this coating hardens, the Pignolata is ready to be served.

(Picture courtesy of Shutterstock other details by Wikipedia)

Cannoli

These are tubes made from pastry which are fried in lard and filled with ricotta cheese and candied peel. Apparently, the name is derived from 'canna' meaning cane sugar, or the barrel of a gun! In Palermo, they are renowned.

(*Courtesy of Shutterstock*)

Granita

This is a well-known semi-frozen dessert of sugar, water, and flavourings, originally from the island, and is commonly assumed to be associated with Messina or Catania. Granita is related to sorbet and Italian ice cream, but in most of Sicily, it has a coarser more crystalline texture. Different freezing techniques create smoother types in a gelato machine, while the coarser varieties are frozen with only occasional agitation, then scraped or shaved.

To be served perhaps after a special family occasion such as a confirmation ceremony shown below?

**Left to Right: Santo and Marianna; Carmella Raia, their daughter;
Grandson Alfonso Roselli; Santos Giuseppe Cusmano;
Santo and Marianna's brother-in-law, Vincenzo Roselli**

SOME POPULAR SICILIAN WINES

1. Malvasia

This wine is bottled near the city of Messina in the North West of the island and is a sweet dessert wine with a full-bodied flavour, similar to Moscato. It is slightly fortified with brandy and looks visually appealing with an iconic yellow colour as it is poured into the glass.

2. Novello

This wine is known for its robust and fruity flavour and has raised awareness of the wide selection of wines that are now on the Island of Sicily. Traditionally, farmers uncork bottles of Novello at the end of the harvesting season.

It is widely regarded as a hearty wine having a complex fruity aroma and dry harmonious flavour. It is produced by means of a 'modern' process using carbon dioxide, depriving the grapes of oxygen to increase rapid alcohol production. Adding yeast to the must (pulp, juice and skin), brings about faster fermentation.

3. Chardonnay

This is now a common name worldwide.

This Sicilian Chardonnay has emerged from the challenge to Sicilian wine producers to do better and compete internationally. To promote this noble and widely popular wine with flavours ranging from sweet to dry.

4. Catarratto Bianco

This wine has a subtle flavour which is appreciated by serious wine drinkers. It can be paired with almost any dinner dish as an excellent white wine that all can enjoy. The perfect complement to fish or chicken, it has been cultivated in Trapani in Eastern Sicily since ancient times and is made from a semi-aromatic grape.

5. Zibibbo

Here is a bolder wine of outstanding flavour and taste which is very popular with Sicilians but which is also appreciated by connoisseurs from abroad. It is often sold alongside Muscatel wines in the marketplace. Its name originates from the Arabic word Zabib meaning raisins, known as the Alexandria Muscat. It has Egyptian origins and the grapes were planted for the first time in Sicily by the Phoenicians over 2,700 years ago and brought into other regions of Europe during the Roman Empire.

6. Grecanico

Grecanico is made from a native Sicilian white grape variety which can be traced back to the colonizing Greeks over 2,700 years ago. This wine has been experiencing a new renaissance among both producers and consumers.

7. Frappato

This is cultivated throughout Sicily and originates in the Syracuse and Ragusa regions. It is a superb robust wine with aromas and flavours of olives, rosemary, Mediterranean herbs and eucalyptus. It is amazing to learn that for many years, Frappato was considered to be a second-class wine, which is only now growing in popularity.

8. Primitivo

This wine is now bottled in Sicily, where it has become a favourite. It is of a quality similar to Zinfandel which is popular in California.

9. Marsala

Marsala is a fortified wine produced near the town of the same name on the south coast of Sicily. It is made with local white grape varietals including Grillo, Inzolia, Catarratto, and Damaschino (although it can also be blended with red grapes.). As with all fortified wine, Marsala is supplemented with a distilled spirit — in this case, usually brandy.

It was first popularized outside Sicily by the English trader John Woodhouse, who, in 1773, landed at the port of Marsala and discovered this local wine. It is still marketed under "Woodhouse", to this day and is added to a popular dish to create Pollo al Marsala (chicken Marsala). It is also the vital ingredient for a dish created in front of hotel restaurant customers, the now-famous **Zabaglione al Marsala.**

This consists of egg yolks and sugar and an eggshell of Marsala wine per customer, gradually whisked over a hot water bath (bain-marie) until firm and then poured into wine glasses prior to serving, accompanied by a small macaroon biscuit and the dessert is designed to be eaten with a teaspoon.

Varieties of Marsala include:

Oro has a golden colour

Ambra - has an amber colour from the *mosto cotto* sweetener added to the wine

Rubino – has a ruby colour, made from red grape varieties

Fine – is aged at least one year

Superiore – is aged at least two years

Superiore Riserva – is aged at least four years

Vergine and/or *Solera* - is aged at least five years

Vergine and/or *Soleras Stravecchio* and *Vergine* and/or *Soleras Riserva* – aged at least ten years.

Wines range from dry to sweet complementing the menu from aperitif to dessert similar to Madeira, Port and Sherry (employing the "Solera System" for blending in the ageing process).

(*Information sourced from Wikipedia and the biographer's personal notes*)

CONCLUSION

Now at the age of eighty-two, Santo Raia can reflect on a lifetime of achievement in a country where he was not born and one very different from his own, as this biography has hopefully conveyed. It could be said that he came to seek a life and work in London, as millions of others from many other countries had done previously, primarily through economic necessity.

This is not so unusual. What is notable, however, is that he has been known and appreciated by hundreds, many with celebrity status, from the theatre, the sporting world and in the legal profession. They have put their trust in him and his son Jack's unique style of hairdressing, in some cases, throughout their entire lives. Their hair has been cut by none other than Santo or his son Jack, and, as devoted clients, they have followed them wherever they have gone. This clientele includes the author of this biography.

As we congratulate Santo, his wife Marianna and their family, including Jack and his wife Ellie, on continuing the business, we should be conscious of the importance of hairdressing as a personal service for maintaining an individual's profile and self-confidence and the role of the dedicated hairdresser in whom clients place their trust and confidence.

ACKNOWLEDGEMENTS

The biographer is very grateful for the kind assistance and encouragement of Keith Aleandri for the editing of these chapters.

To Santo, Jack and Ellie Raia for the provision of essential pictures and photographs to enhance the written account and also the kind assistance of granddaughter Cinzia and Rosario Roselli for the provision of Sicilian dishes.

To Peter Such for his patience with editing and creative ideas.